Mozart
The Man and His Music

Linda Pearson-Adams

Rosen REAL READERS

Rosen Classroom Books and Materials
New York

Published in 2002 by The Rosen Publishing Group, Inc.
29 East 21st Street, New York, NY 10010

Book Design: Haley Wilson

Photo Credits: Cover, pp. 1, 3, 4, 6, 8, 10, 14, 15, 16 © Archive Photo; pp. 12–13 © Corbis.

ISBN: 0-8239-8227-0
6-pack ISBN: 0-8239-8630-6

Manufactured in the United States of America

Contents

Mozart and His Father

Wolfgang Amadeus (ah-muh-DAY-uhs) Mozart was born in 1756 in Austria (AW-stree-uh), a country in Europe. Mozart's father was a **musician** (myoo-ZIH-shen). He taught Mozart everything he knew about music.

Mozart learned how to play music by watching his father play. He and his father often played music together.

Allegretto

unbekant, es war ein herzigs Veilchen. Da kam ein' junge

-her die Wiese her, und sang.

Blume der Natur, ach nur — ein kleines Weilchen bis mich das

A Special Child

Mozart began playing music when he was very young. By the time he was five years old, he knew how to play the **organ**, the piano, and the **violin** very well. He also began to write his own music. His first pieces of music were played in public when he was only six years old!

Mozart wrote this piece of music, "The Violet," in 1785, but he may have written his first piece of music when he was only four years old!

Young Mozart

Mozart did not live like other children. As a child and teenager, Mozart traveled around Europe with his father. Mozart gave many **concerts** to show off his talent and earn money. During this time, Mozart wrote more and more music.

Mozart wrote a lot of his music to be played on the piano.

Mozart's Operas

Mozart wrote twenty-two **operas**. An opera is a play that has music to go along with the story. The actors sing most of the words. Some of Mozart's operas are funny, and some are very sad. Today, people still go to see many of Mozart's operas.

One of Mozart's most famous operas is called *The Magic Flute*.

Mozart's Symphonies

Mozart also wrote more than forty **symphonies** (SIM-fuh-nees). A symphony is a long piece of music. It is played by many musicians playing different kinds of musical **instruments** together.

Mozart's most famous symphony, Number 41, is sometimes called the *Jupiter*.

Mozart wrote his first symphonies when he was only eight or nine years old. Today, orchestras still play Mozart's symphonies.

A Short Life

Mozart died in 1791 after a long illness. He was only thirty-five years old, but he had already written more than 600 pieces of music. Mozart's music was his gift to the world.

Glossary

concert A musical show put on for the public.

instrument Something used to make music.

musician A person who sings, plays, or writes music.

opera A play in which the actors sing most of the words.

organ A musical instrument that looks and is played much like a piano.

symphony A long piece of music that is written for many musicians to play.

violin A wooden instrument with strings that is played with a bow.

Index